CHAMPIONS ARE FORGED IN FIRE

MORGAN FULLER

2019 Copyright © Morgan Fuller
ISBN: 9780578499574

Table of Contents

Foreword 7
Introduction 9
Releasing Anger 10
Freedom Fighter 12
He Never Fails 14
I Believe 18
Do You Love Them? 22
I Trust Your Heart 24
Friend of God 26
Overcomer 28
Unshaken 30
Live Limitless 32
Character Matters 34
You Were Made For This 36
You Are 38
Love Has A Name 42
Trusting Father's Heart 44
Don't Give Up Now 46
Truth Over Me 48
Keep Moving Forward 50
Revive Me, O Lord 51
The Son Still Shines 52
Never Too Late 53
The King of Glory Lives 54
While I Wait 56
What A Time 58
How Can It Be? 60
I Am 62
Come Away With Me 64
What If? 66
Come Alive 68
Hope Is 70

Foreword

by Apostle Ken Malone

I love poems, psalms, proverbs and parables. Poems bring peace, happiness, fullness of joy and the like. The purpose of a poem is to bring change in your inner man. When a poem is written within the integrity of Christ's word, it changes a person from the inside out. This type of writing unlocks the heart of the reader to experience Christ in a new way. I wish there were more books written like this. Morgan Fuller has done a great job in unlocking Heaven's resources to you and I.

As you read this book of prophetic poems and psalms, you are going to be drawn into a fuller reality of how the Lord embraces you as His child. Also, three things will begin to align in your life: relationship, discipleship and identity. Your life will now begin to unlock as a Champion and one who has been forged in fire.

Relationship

From the beginning of time when the Lord made Adam and Eve, He made them so He could have relationship with them and that man could have relationship with one another. Relationship is in jeopardy today as the enemy of our soul wars against our relationship with God and with one another. Meditation on Him and His word through poems, enables you to slow down, breath and take pause to love and appreciate all that God has put you into relationship with. As you read a poem in this book, pause and meditate on what you have just read. Ask the Lord, how do I apply this? Slow down a little and fall in love with your first love, Jesus Christ. As you do, His presence will come on you and bring you peace.

Discipleship

The cost of following Christ is worth the price. Laying down your life and taking up His will gives you access into the third Heaven. Jesus said, "If any man comes after Me, let him deny himself and take up his cross and follow Me." (See Matthew 16:24) This is the kind of God living that puts you into the Heavenly realm. In the heavens is were Christ is seated, far above all principality and power. (See Ephesians 1:20-21) When you begin to follow Him as a disciple, He also places you with Him in the heavens. (See Ephesians 1:5-6)

As you read these poems, you will begin to discover gold nuggets or pearls of great price. Pick those up and beginning following Christ. Be one of His disciples.

Identity

Many today have lost their way and cannot seem to find who they truly are. As I was reading "Champions Are Forged In Fire," I started to see a pattern that the Lord was writing through Morgan. That pattern is His identity within you. When God made Adam and Eve, He made them to have His image and His likeness. He made them to have dominion, to subdue and to be fruitful. (See Genesis 1:26-28) That identity has not changed. His plans for you are to be like Him.

As you read, "Champions Are Forged In Fire," build relationship with Him, become one of His disciples and find your identity in Christ.

Ken Malone
Forerunner Ministries

Introduction

Here I am again in awe of what God has done. It doesn't matter how many times The Father comes through on His word, I am amazed every single time. Again and again, He shows up in a mighty way. He always keeps His word and always in a way for our greatest good and His greatest glory. The impossible is made possible with Him.

But, as the title of this book suggests, it's not always a walk in the park for us. Champions don't happen by chance. They don't accidentally become champions or stumble upon it. Champions are built. They are made carefully. They are forged. This book of poems reflects just that.

The crucible of life's trials and obstacles grow ordinary people like us into extraordinary examples of God's goodness and power. The fire will be hot, the smoke thick, and the flame bright. But you, my friend, will come out strong, powerful, and balanced by the Master Craftsman.

Let this life and your experiences forge you into the champion God has called you to be. Let these poems encourage you along the way. Don't give up and don't leave the fire only partially refined. You are designed to be a champion. You are being forged by the fire.

Releasing Anger

I could hold onto anger
Or I could let it go
And reach with free hands
For the promises and blessings You have for me.

What good does anger do me
Even if I have a right to it
Anger brittles the bones
It's a cancer to body and spirit

Lord, help me surrender this anger
Surrender it to Your sovereign plan
Help me leave it at the foot of Your cross
To be free from it and released from its grip

Teach me to replace anger with forgiveness
To release and bless those who have hurt me
Teach me how to choose to forgive
Let me not keep a record of wrongs

Remind me of the forgiveness You have given me
Even the things I thought were unforgivable
Let love, not anger, be my character
And love be my reaction to injury

Teach me to love unconditionally
And when blows to my heart come
Let love be my first response

Because love builds where anger destroys
And love unites where anger divides
Love covers where anger exposes
And love gives grace when anger condemns

Let my character reflect my Savior
When troubles come
And let me respond rightly
When circumstances are overwhelming

Empty me of myself
And fill me with Your Spirit
I know people are watching
Lord, let them see You

Freedom Fighter

I am a rebel
I choose to stand for what is right
And against corrupt systems of this world

I choose to walk away from religion
Into the freedom God offers

I will not keep quiet while watching people I love
Live in bondage to religious chains
Disguised as tradition and reverence

I will raise my voice to declare the Word of The Lord
Deliver a call to holiness and freedom from sin

Too many are tied down with strongholds created by our enemy
A wolf in sheep's clothing
Deceiving them to believe they have all these rules
Rules to keep to be Holy
When it is love and grace that brings repentance
And changes the desires and actions of a soul

My fight is with principalities and powers
That would try to oppress God's people

My cause is to see nations won by God's love
And living in His peace

I am a freedom fighter
I give my life to see others made whole
To carry the gospel to the hurting and broken

To challenge and resist the lies of our enemy
To bring every heart hope
And to live a life worthy of the calling

Let religion
Tradition
And bondage
Say what they will of me

Rebellious
Out of control
Too wild
Irreverent

I will become even more than this
To see The Kingdom of Heaven brought to Earth

Come Lord Jesus
Shake our churches awake
Open the eyes of the blinded

Here I am, Lord
Send me

I will suffer the cause
To see Your Kingdom come

Send me

He Never Fails

I called
And He answered

I cried out from my pit
And God reached down to pull me out

I made the journey home
And The Father came running to meet me

He did not turn a blind eye to my plight
Pretend to not see the pain I was in

He did not turn a deaf ear to my cries
Act like He had not heard my suffering

Our God is kind and He is faithful
He is gracious and full of mercy

As sure as I am of His love for me
I am sure of His love for you

He will not abandon you
And He will not leave you in the pit

Your current crisis is not too much for Him to fix
Your mistakes are not too many for His redemption

Jesus has already paid that price
He has already made your way

You are greatly loved by The King of all

We are highly favored children
Members of a Kingdom that surpasses time

Will He not see to it His Children's needs are met?
Will He not supply it all?

This weeping may endure for the night
But His joy comes in the morning

Though it may seem He is four days too late
He always arrives right on time
Who are we to think Our Father is not on His way?

What He has said He will do
He is faithful to see it done.

He is the protector of His promise to you.
Neither famine or drought can take it.

Our God is faithful to complete every good work He began
He has not forgotten you
And He will not leave His promises to you unkept

Don't dismay, Beloved
The God who loves you will meet you where you are
And He cares too much to leave you there

Do not fret
He will always come through for you

You can trust Him
You can count on Him
He will never disappoint
And He will never leave you

GOD HEARS YOU
GOD SEES YOU
AND GOD WILL NOT FORSAKE YOU

NOT BECAUSE OF WHO YOU ARE
BUT BECAUSE OF WHO HE IS
HE IS A GOOD FATHER

REST IN THIS
HE IS NEVER FAR AWAY
AND HE WILL NEVER FAIL YOU

I Believe

I believe everyone is born with purpose

Dreamed up in the heart of God for great things

I believe God never sent a single soul to earth for just existing

I believe there is no darkness too thick God's light can't penetrate

And no pit too deep for Him to pull us out of

I believe no bad thing can overcome the righteous

I believe God when He says I will never be forsaken by Him

I believe we have authority as children of The Most High

To take back what the enemy has stolen from us

To receive good gifts from our Father

And change the atmosphere wherever we put our feet

I believe God has a whole lot of new and wonderful ready to pour out for us

I believe we are nowhere near powerless against the attacks and circumstances that try to overtake us

I believe we can see the goodness of God in the land of the living

I BELIEVE THE FINISHED WORK OF JESUS SETS US FREE

AND MADE A WAY FOR US

I BELIEVE ABUNDANT LIFE IS OUR BIRTHRIGHT

I BELIEVE WE CAN LIVE A LIFE FULLY AWAKE

I BELIEVE WE CAN DO ALL THINGS THROUGH CHRIST WHO GIVES US STRENGTH

AND WE CAN DO NOTHING APART FROM HIM

I BELIEVE IT IS GOD WHO ORDERS THE STEPS OF THE RIGHTEOUS

I BELIEVE OUR RIGHTEOUSNESS IS ONLY BECAUSE OF CHRIST WITHIN US

I BELIEVE WORSHIP IS A POWERFUL WEAPON OF WARFARE

I BELIEVE PRAYER WORKS

I BELIEVE THE SOUND OF OUR VOICES CAN SHAKE THE GATES OF HELL

I BELIEVE THE FIRE IN OUR BONES NEVER HAS TO FLICKER OUT

I BELIEVE WE NEVER HAVE TO LOWER THE STANDARD FOR COMFORTS SAKE

OR TO MAKE OTHERS FEEL OKAY IN THEIR COMPLACENCY

I BELIEVE THE CROSS WAS MEANT TO OFFEND THE OFFENSIVE PLACES INSIDE OF US and meant to change wickedness to holiness

I believe we don't have to live in bondage to sin

I believe we can change the world for the Kingdom of God

I believe God is always for us and never against us

I believe every word the Bible says

I believe God wants to use us to accomplish His work in the Earth

I believe we can see the power of God manifest on the Earth through signs, wonders, and miracles.

I believe we can witness His glory if we only ask

I believe The Father is leaning over His throne to breathe in our praise

I believe we never have to settle for defeat

I believe God already has a strategy for our victory over the enemy

I believe we can have intimate relationship with The Father

I believe God has a plan for us so big we can't even begin to comprehend

I believe God has placed a dream inside each of us and is cheering from the Throne, "Go. Go. GO!"

I believe God wants to show us every day how much He loves us

I believe God's mercies are new every morning

I believe we can hear God's voice if we will just listen for it.

I believe Holy Spirit wants to tell us the secrets of Heaven

I believe people need to see the love of Jesus in us

I believe there are souls waiting for us to do what God has called us to

Waiting for us to live the gospel and share the good news of grace

I believe if we can just get the Kingdom that's inside of us out of us, the world would look a whole lot different

I believe the greatest message we carry is the message of hope and freedom through Jesus Christ

I believe Jesus saves, sets free, and delivers

And I believe the best is just beginning

Do You Love Them?

Today's media will tell you to put down your weapons and love one another
Let people live how they please
Keep your words to yourself
That tolerance will bring peace

But real love fights for truth
And peace is never won by silent protest

Open your mouths and call darkness what it is
Reveal truth and mercy that cleanses

Do you love them enough to share the truth of the gospel?
That we were also lost and undone
But Jesus suffered, died, and rose so we can be made whole
So we all can live free from the curse

Do you love them enough to go to war for their deliverance?
To pick up the sword of The Spirit and cut down the lies of the enemy?

I can't sit silently while they run into hell
And call it keeping the peace

I can't stay quiet
And deceive myself into believing tolerance is love

Will you stand for all this evil in the world
By deciding it's someone else's problem?

It is not spewing hate to deliver truth!

And it is not love to do nothing when so many are bound to sin!

Quiet, Docile, and stagnant Christianity was never God's intention for you!

Do you love them enough to speak up?

Are you willing to stay in this war so they can be free?

Do you love them enough to get down in the pit to help them climb out?

Are you too concerned with getting your hands dirty that you would let them die?

Do you love them enough to pick up your weapons to fight hell for them?

Can you choose to see what Jesus sees in them?

Do you love them enough to expose the liar for who he is and introduce them to the Savior?

Do you love them enough to see them set free?

Do you love them enough?

I Trust Your Heart

When I feel alone
Abandoned
And rejected by man
Let me hear You singing over me
Remind me who You say I am
And show me again Your great love for me

In disappointment and hurt
Let me feel Your presence
Comfort Your daughter
Restore peace to my soul

Though man may forget
You never do
You hold every moment
And You catch every tear

You collect them in bottles
And You alone give beauty for ashes
Let my hurting heart offer praise to You,
King of Heaven

It's not pretty
And it's a little broken
But I know you make broken things beautiful
In Your time

In my moment of need
I know you are not far from me
I take refuge under Your wings
And I trust Your heart
I trust in your love for me

Sing over me again
Let the sound of Your voice resonate in my soul
Bringing rest and peace
Speak over me, Your Word
That brings joy to my heart

You are the comforter
You will turn my mourning into dancing
I wait patiently for You to keep your promise
You always keep your promises

And while I wait
I will offer what I possess
It's all Yours

I know You will work it all for my good
And for Your glory
You never forget me
I never escape Your gaze
Your thoughts toward me are too many to count
Your love heals my heart

Though I may cry for a time
I know that joy is coming
I trust Your heart
I trust in Your love for me

Your promises are true
You never fail to keep them
You speak truth
And You do not lie to me

Jesus,
I trust Your heart.

Friend of God

Let my heart become an ark to house Your presence
An altar where sweet perfumes of worship flow

Set this heart ablaze with love for You, O God
And make it pure like fresh fallen snow

Refine the impurities from this vessel
Cleanse my lips so I can speak Your Name
Sing your praises for the entirety of my days

Meet with me awhile, Lord
Come and share Your time with me

My desire is to know You more

My request is to be found in Your presence
To be known for loving You

Let my reputation in the throne room hold greater weight
Than my reputation with man

Let my mind be ever set on Kingdom things

Teach me to walk in Your ways, O God
And to lead a life that reflects your heart

Let me be known
Not for what I profess
But for Whom I serve

Let me represent You well

Above all, Lord
Let me be known by You

Let my name be
Friend of God

Overcomer

I have been where you are
But I have overcome
By the power of Jesus
And the word of my testimony
Because of this
I can tell you
You were made to overcome this
You were made to stand victorious
Beside our Victor, Christ Jesus
You were created for a war that you will not lose
Battles that will only make you stronger
Stronger in faith
In perseverance
In love
And in obedience to God
You were made for this day and hour
To reflect the Kingdom
To show the world what they were made for
Made to shift atmospheres wherever you go
To set the world on fire
For the God who laid His life down for them
You were made to leave prophetic seed
In cities
In regions
And in nations all over the world
Made to cultivate a Kingdom culture here on the Earth

You were made to live free
So you can lead others to freedom
Choose to live in the freedom God has won for you
Don't let the enemy lie to you, Dear Friends
He will do his best to make you believe you are not enough
You can't overcome
That you will stay in this pit forever
Let me deliver this word to you
God made you for this war
And He sent Jesus to win your victory
Don't faint
Don't throw in the towel
Do not give in
You were born for victory
You were born to overcome
Stand up
Stand tall
You are an overcomer

Unshaken

When the ground around me is shaking

And I'm unsure it can hold me steady

I know You keep me secure

When I can stand on nothing else

I can stand firm on Your word

I can place my trust in Your unchanging nature

You are faithful

And You are just

Your love is irrevocable

And Your promises are unfailing

God of all my days

I will hope in You alone

Father of all fathers

King above all kings

I rest at Your holy feet

I place my life in Your hands

They are more than capable

When the winds and waves rage

When the sands shift beneath my feet

When the fire roars around me

And the pressure seems too much to bear

I am securely seated on the Solid Rock

I am held firmly by the Living God

I will not be shaken

Live Limitless

Women of God
I have come with a message for you
A word from The Lord
Declaring over you who you were made to be

You were created soft
But not fragile

Delicate
But not frail

Feminine
But not weak

You were created with emotions
Not to be ruled by them

You were created to have a gentle and quiet spirit
But a bold and powerful voice

The only limits you have to complete the call
Are the limits you allow to be placed on your shoulders

The cycle of timid, afraid, restricted women stops here Today
In this room

And the generational legacy of bold, powerful, limitless
women begins with you

Throw off the cloaks that mark you as a beggar at the gate
And run through the city declaring He has made you whole

You are on Earth for such a time as this

Will you shrink back ruled by fear?
Or will you rise knowing the Lion of Judah goes with you?

Choose in this moment
To live as you were created to be

Bold
Powerful
And without chains

Choose to shatter society's glass ceilings
To shake up the status quo
To be a bold force for the Kingdom of God

The next generation is depending on you
They are looking to your example
Choose to live limitless

Character Matters

My desire is to manifest the character of Jesus in my life

To exhibit His behaviors in every circumstance and situation
In every single moment of my time on this Earth

Holy Spirit
Teach me to walk in Your ways
Lead me step by step
In each and every trait

In Wisdom
Don't let my zeal outrun You
Teach me to steward passion well

In Peace
Come rest upon my mind
Keep my thoughts steadfast on Christ

In Joy
Fill my soul and mouth with praise
Overflow from my heart like a fountain

In Compassion
Help me to see others as You do
Let me be the hands and feet of Jesus in this hour

In Hope
Overtake the doubt and drive me to keep going
Don't allow me to give up when breakthrough is just around the corner

In Patience
Teach me to endure the process
Help me to hold on until the promise comes

In Holiness
Set me apart
Make me a bride without spot or wrinkle

In Gentleness
Guide my response in every situation
Let my words be honey
Sweet to hear and pleasant to receive

In Kindness
Fill my eyes with mercy
And my hands with generosity

In Humility
Let me prefer others over myself
Help me to remain the woman in the middle
Reaching forward to the wisdom ahead of me
And behind to raise up the next generation

In Love
Fill my mouth with words that share Your grace
Let my actions convey Your love that heals the broken
Frees the bound
And Delivers the oppressed

Father
Let my legacy be one that points to You
Let my life declare Your goodness
And Let my reputation bring glory to Your Name alone

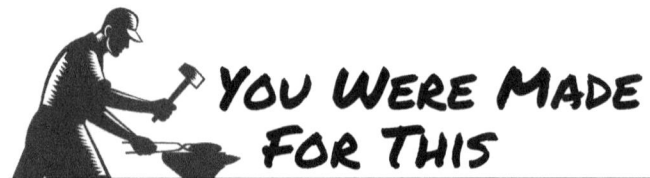

You Were Made For This

You were created for intimacy with God
Close relationship
Constant communion
Created to host His presence

You were made for a life flowing from the secret place
To be known in the throne room of Heaven
Made to be called Friend of God

You were created to shake nations
To manifest the Kingdom of God on earth
Change the tide in your region
Yes
You were made for this

Shaping history was not just for generals of times passed
You were created to be used of God
To redeem current times through intercession
You were born for such a time as this

Don't miss your calling
Because you've neglected meeting with Father God

Do not just exist
Live worthy of the high calling on your life

Stay steadfast and faithful to Him who had called you redeemed
And you will not go astray

Water the garden of your soul with His Word
And you will not fail to meet your mark

Our Father wants to revive your life daily
But He can't do that if you choose to ignore His call to
come away with Him

He can't nourish your spirit
If you choose to grow complacent in the place of prayer

Be found at His feet
And do all you were created to

Seek intimacy with God
And flourish in every area of your life

Be present in His presence
You were born for relationship
You were created to live life with God
You were made for this.

You Are

You ask me
"Who do you say that I am?"

I say
You are Father
Healer
Restorer
And Defender

You are Holy
Righteous
Just
And Victorious

You are Redeemer
Provider
Deliverer
And Judge

You are Counselor
Jehovah
Emmanuel
And Friend

When I ask You
"Who do You say that I am?"

You say
I am Your daughter
Beloved
Cherished
And Held

I AM HEALED
SANCTIFIED
REDEEMED
AND BLESSED

I AM COVERED
MADE RIGHTEOUS
PROVIDED FOR
AND LOVED

I AM VICTORIOUS
DELIVERED
FAVORED
AND FOREVER FREE

I AM YOUR CHILD
AND YOU ARE MY FATHER

I AM YOUR SERVANT
AND YOU ARE MY MASTER

I AM YOUR FRIEND
AND YOU ARE MY GOD

YOU ARE THE KEEPER OF YOUR PROMISES
AND THE COMPLETER OF YOUR GOOD WORK

YOU ARE THE ONLY FAITHFUL ONE
AND THE PROVIDER OF ALL MY NEEDS

YOU SING OVER ME WITH GLADNESS
AND YOU ARE THE BANNER THAT GOES BEFORE ME

You are my Victorious King
And You are The Lover of my soul

You are my Healer
And You are my Refuge

You are the Everlasting God
The Bright and Morning Star

You are The Alpha and Omega
The Beginning and The End

You rule and reign
On The Earth and in Heaven

You are Almighty God
And You will walk with me in the valley and on the mountain top

You go before me in all my endeavors
And You will order each and every step

You protect me on every side
And You stand with me in the flame

You strengthen me for battle
And You are my shield and sword

You are the Eternal One
I give you all the glory

Love Has a Name

There is a light at the end of the tunnel
An end to this depression you are trapped in
There is light flooding your dark corridor

Hope is chasing you down
Love is chasing you down
Love has a name
And His Name is Jesus

He is not satisfied to leave you like He found you
He is not content to let you stay in the pit
His love for you is too great for Him to stand for mediocrity
And too strong for Him to watch you suffer

Don't give up just before the dawn
Don't let go before The Son delivers His promise to you

Jesus never fails
And He never forgets what He said He will do

Our Father is a good father
And He does not delight in our desperation
Rather he rejoices in pouring out blessings
Blessings that we cannot contain

Holy Spirit is a constant companion to you
You are never alone

Just persevere
Trust the process
He will not allow you to be made a fool
And He is faithful beyond compare

Hope has seen you
Love has heard you
Love has a name
And His Name is Jesus

Trusting Father's Heart

Rest is warfare

And rest is found in Your presence

The surety of knowing I don't have to strive

You have made the way straight before me

Days and nights

They pass before You

And You order the hours to them all

You order my steps the same

I will not fear the future

It is already held in Your mighty hands

And Your plan is to prosper me

Uncertainty will not deter me

When I can not see Your face

I will trust Your heart

You do not forget me

Or leave me in a dark place
You walk with me through the valley
And lead me to the mountain top
Your deep wells sustain me in the desert
And in the meadow
You are the light that brightens my days
And you are the compass that directs my way
Jesus
Of this I am sure
You have nothing but good for me
So,
When I can not see Your face
I will trust Your heart.

Don't Give Up Now

You have to keep moving

You've got to keep going

Push through the pain

Trust that God's love will sustain

Persevere through the ache

Even when your heart feels like it might break

His promise endures

And He holds you secure

There is no obstacle that can stop you

No valley He won't bring you through

Our unstoppable God is on your side

He is making a way

He is turning the tide

Don't quit now

You are almost there

Just a few more steps

I know you can make it

I know you won't fail

Your promise is just on the other side
I know things may look dark
But the light is just beyond your sight
Don't stop where you are
Please
Stay in the fight
Don't give up now

Truth Over Me

No matter how things appear

I am NOT abandoned

And I am NEVER alone

You are ever before me

Behind me

And beside me

In Your great goodness

You supply my every need

You fulfill my every longing

Though the enemy whispers

I am not wanted and I have no place

You continue to sing truth over me

I CHOOSE to hold to truth

I am not isolated from my peers

And I am not tossed to the side

I AM loved

I AM valued

And I AM wanted among the people of God

Like Moses

When I can no longer hold my arms up

You, O God
Will send people to my aid
Friends to hold me secure
You will send forth a message full of hope
You have placed the right people in my life
People to hold me up on every side
I am **NOT** abandoned
I have this assurance
You have **NEVER** left me
And You will never leave me lonely
I am surrounded by You and Your people
I am loved by Your people
And I am loved by You

Keep Moving Forward

These obstacles in front of you
They are just illusions
Distractions sent by the enemy to hinder you
Keep Moving Forward

Your destiny is just beyond your sight
It's waiting for you
Stay obedient
Stay the course
Keep Moving Forward

There is nothing that can stop
What God has called to come forth
His word is forever settled in Heaven

God said your promise is coming
Satan cannot stop it
Trust the heart of your Father
Keep Moving Forward

Now is the time
Walk out your God-given calling
Go after all He has said is for you
Keep Moving Forward

Don't stop
Don't slow down
Keep Moving Forward

Revive Me, O Lord

Raise this dead heart to life again
Will it to beat and it will obey
New life to replace death
Years of hurt and loss have hardened what You created
Soften it once again with Your love
Change stone to flesh
Give breathe
And hope
And life
Rain down on the dry and thirsty places of this soul
Oh that you would revive me again
Revive me,
O Lord

The Son Still Shines

In the pain and heartache
In the sorrow and sickness
The sun still shines

Bitterness and loss
Hurt and despair
The sun still shines

Every moment of anger
Every moment of doubt
The sun still shines

Steady as the beating war drum
Warm as sand beside the ocean
The sun still shines

Gray clouds may cover you
Rain my blur your vision
But the sun still shines

Lift up your head
Feel the rays of forgiveness and love
The Son still shines

Love covers every spot
Redemption pays every debt
And The Son still shines

Deliverance is here
Salvation is here
And The Son still shines

Never Too Late

*In the grave four long days
And what it seems is
I'll spend my eternity here
But I know that He is coming
Yes
I know He is on His way
The people around me
They are all mourning
Believing I've been left to turn to dust
Won't they be surprised when Jesus shows up
He is surely on His way
I know He is coming
I am not dead in the grave
Waiting for a savior who never comes
I am simply sleeping
Resting until He shows up
It may look like I've been left where I lay
But my God is on His way
Friend
If you feel like you've been left for dead
If it looks like you've been left where you lay
Do not trust in what your eyes may see
It may look like Jesus is four days too late
But that is simply not the case
Dear friend
Rest in this
He is never too late
Your God is surely on His way*

The King of Glory Lives

When they hung Him there

I thought it was all over

All my hopes had been dashed

And they had killed my only chance of redemption

They killed my beloved

When they put His lifeless body in that tomb

My heart shattered into splintered pieces

And I sobbed bitter tears

A stone covering my freedom

My healing

My Deliverer

But Sunday came

And when I went to grieve at His tomb again

I was met by a view so stunning and glorious

No one believed me when I told them

But they soon saw for themselves

The tomb was empty

Those heavenly hosts told me
He is alive
He had risen
And with Him all my hopes and healing
He got up from that grave
And set the whole world free

Jesus lives and breathes
Now He reigns forever
From the throne of Heaven
The King of Glory is alive
My Redeemer lives

While I Wait

How long must I wait for my promises to manifest?

And how long will my prayers be filled with bitter tears?

My soul cries out and my heart aches for longings to be fulfilled.

But I know my God is faithful
And I know He is working everything out
For His glory
And for my good

So while I wait in the valley of transition

I will exalt the Name of The Lord

While I stand in expectation for the promises of God

I will praise Him who is seated on the Throne of Heaven

You alone
O Lord
Hold each moment

You are above all
And worthy to be praised

You cover me with Your wings
And You sing over me with gladness

My hope will not be in vain

I trust You, God
Your promises are surely on the way to me

Not much longer now
I can see them there in the distance

So while I wait just a little while more
I will praise the Name of The Lord

What A Time

Can you hear it?
The sound of rain
Glory poured out over the earth
It's a flood rushing in
Outpouring that cannot be contained

What can hold back a move of God?
What can hinder His Spirit?

Oh what a wonderful joy it is to be a part of His plan!

What a time to be living in!

How humbling to be used of God

How awe-inspiring to see Him change our world

Can you see it?
The trees and grass become more green
The rivers rise and the sun shines brighter
It's creation responding to Holy Spirit's call
Life rising out of ashes

Oh what a sight to behold!

What a great and powerful God we serve!

That He wants us to a be a part

To use us in a move on the earth

Can you feel it?
The rumblings of revival across the land
The shaking of change
Strongholds crashing down

Oh what a glorious unfolding!

What a miraculous unveiling!

It's a brand new day
Full of beauty and wonder

Our great God is on the move
And we get to see His mighty hand

Our God is renewing the land
And we are privileged to watch it all

What a time to be alive!

Do you see it?
Do you hear it?
Open your eyes and see what God is showing us

How Can It Be?

Desperate

Scavenging

Desolate

That is my life without You, Lord

Hurting and broken

Hunger and thirst

So lost without You, Lord

You picked me up

Cleaned and clothed me

Made a way home

Lit a path for me to see

Unworthy to even carry Your sandals

You bestowed upon this life a mantle

A calling

Full of Kingdom purpose

How can it be?

A WRETCH SUCH AS ME
GIVEN THE PRIVILEGE OF KING'S
AND AUTHORITY OF PRINCES
GIFTED WITH YOUR HOLY SPIRIT
AND LOVED BY THE MOST HIGH GOD

I AM LEFT IN BREATHTAKING AWE
OH WHAT A LOVE THIS IS!
THAT YOU WOULD WANT A LOWLY BEING SUCH AS ME

HOW CAN IT BE?

I AM

I AM **NOT** AFRAID
I AM STRONG
I AM BRAVE
I AM CAPABLE

I AM **NOT** INTIMIDATED
I AM CONFIDENT
I AM SECURE
I AM AS BOLD AS A LION

I AM **NOT** CONDEMNED
I AM LOVED
I AM FORGIVEN
I AM REDEEMED

I AM **NOT** ORPHANED
I AM A DAUGHTER
I AM ANOINTED
I AM SEATED AT THE KING'S TABLE

I AM **NOT** ENSLAVED
I AM RESCUED
I AM ALIVE
I AM FREE

I AM **NOT** ABANDONED
I AM HELD
I AM WANTED
I AM RESTING IN GOD'S PRESENCE

I AM **NOT** A LOST CAUSE
I AM RESTORED
I AM VALUED
I AM A PART OF HIS KINGDOM

I AM NOT BOUND
I AM WILD
I AM DELIVERED
I AM DANCING FOR HIS GLORY

I AM NOT IN LAST PLACE
I AM A FORERUNNER
I AM RUNNING AFTER GOD
I AM GOING TO FINISH MY RACE WELL

I AM NOT ALONE
I AM COVERED
I AM SURRENDERED
I AM LOVED BY GOD AND HIS PEOPLE

I AM NOT IMPOVERISHED
I AM BLESSED
I AM FAVORED
I AM PROVIDED FOR BY MY GOD

I AM A CHILD OF THE LIVING GOD
LOVED, HELD, AND FAVORED IN ALL THINGS
SAFE, SHELTERED, AND SECURE IN HIS MIGHTY HANDS
I AM FOUND IN HIS COURTS
AND I AM LOVED BY THE KING

Come Away With Me

Come away with Me
My love for you overflows
It is unending
And it is unquenchable
There is no height or depth it cannot reach

Come away with Me
There is no need to beg for connection
I am always near
And I always hear you

Come away with Me
We will dance and sing
Open your heart and receive My love for you
Let Me satisfy the longing of your soul

Come away with Me
My heart longs for your company
To meet with you awhile
Let's spend some time together
Just the two of us

Come away with Me, My Beloved
Let Me shower you with My affections
Let Me fill you up to overflowing
Let Me rest peace upon your shoulders
Place a crown of righteousness upon your head

Come away with Me, My Love
Come away with Me

WHAT IF?

What would happen if we lived in revival?
What would our cities look like?

They would look like empty orphanages
And made up hospital beds
Vacant jail cells
And restored marriages
There would be worship in the streets
And we would see miracles at every turn

What if we prayed and trusted God to do the work we contend for?
What if we picked up our mustard seed and weren't afraid to use it?

We would see hope restored
We would see captives go free

What if we opened our Bible and believed it?
Read God's promises to us and didn't question that He would keep them?

Fear would have no hold
Nations would shake
Demons would flee
And God's glory would flood the earth

What if we believed Jesus when He said we would be given power and authority?
If we walked in faith and obedience to the call of Christ
We would see our region
Our nation
Changed

What if we weren't scared?
If we quit telling Holy Spirit to be quiet in our services?

What if we lived wild?
What if we lived like we believe the Bible?

What if?

Come Alive

Come alive, Church
Our God is not dead
Stale or plastic
Our God is not bored
Tired or sleeping
So why are we?

Get up!
Get moving!
Because He lives so do you!
Because He is powerful so are you!

Revival should be bubbling on the inside of you!
Rise up in authority
Declare revival come to your city!

We have revival within us
Why are we stowing it away?
Why do we sit quietly?

You can't bring life to your region
If you are walking around like the dead

Wake up you sleeper!
It is past time to move
Sound the early morning bells
Awaken the dawn with rejoicing

Believers
Flood the streets with His glory
Be carriers of His presence
Revival should be flowing in our city
Jesus did not save us for ourselves

Worship with wild abandon
Sing praise unto The Lord

How will the world know there is freedom
If we hide it while we live among them?

Live in the open
Live out loud

Revival is simply this
Sons and daughters
Seeking, finding, and reuniting
Lost sons and daughters with The Father

Revival is loving as Jesus loved
Living as Jesus lived

Revival is true freedom
Revival is a culture
It's our culture

It's the fire inside of us!

Revival is our birthright
And ours to freely share

Awaken this city
Shake the gates
Shout it from the rooftops
Testify in the valleys
This land shall live
This land thrives
Because God's presence hovers here

Let all people hear a roar
Declaring the coming King

Come alive, Church
Come alive

Hope Is

Hope is the yellow sunshine
Beaming on your face
The warmth of summer heat's embrace

Hope is bright green grass
Lush and vibrant
New life sprouting from the ground as evidence

Hope is blue ocean water
Deep and vast
The steady rhythmic washing away of the past

Hope is raging orange fire
Burning up what's dead
Refining that which lives inside your head

Hope is crimson red
The blood of our precious Savior
Flowing down Calvary's tree

Hope is blinding white
An angelic host declaring
"Jesus is no longer here.
He is not dead but lives!"

Hope died
Rose
And now lives forevermore

Hope is Jesus Christ
And His completed work

Hope is God, the Father
And relationship with Him restored

Hope is Holy Spirit
Daily communion with Him

Hope is living in love
Acting in mercy
And walking humbly with our God

ABOUT THE AUTHOR

MORGAN FULLER is happily married to her best friend, Eric Fuller. Together they strive to raise their daughters, Rhylee Jane and Anna Claire, to love and live for Jesus radically and unapologetically. Morgan currently serves on the leadership team for ROAR Church Texarkana and is a member of ROAR Apostolic Network. She desires to see people set free and living wild for The Lord. Her heart's cry is to give voice back to the Church and to declare the goodness of God all the days of her life.

www.ingramcontent.com/pod-product-compliance
Lightning Source LLC
Chambersburg PA
CBHW070304010526
44108CB00039B/1812